CREATIVE USES · FOR RECYCLABLES ·

175 Easy-to-Do
THANKSGIVING
CRAFTS

Edited by Sharon Dunn Umnik

BOYDS MILLS PRESS
Honesdale, Pennsylvania

Inside this book...
you'll find a fabulous assortment of crafts made from
recyclable items and inexpensive things found in
or around your house. Have pencils, crayons,
scissors, tape, paintbrushes, and other supplies for
craft making close by. —*the Editor*

Boyds Mills Press, Inc.
815 Church Street
Honesdale, Pennsylvania 18431
Printed in China

Publisher Cataloging-in-Publication Data
175 easy-to-do Thanksgiving crafts : creative uses for recyclables / edited by
Sharon Dunn Umnik.—1st ed.
[64]p. : col. ill. ;   cm.
Summary : Includes step-by-step directions to make craft items such as
Pilgrims, holiday-table accessories, turkeys, and more.
ISBN-13: 978-1-56397-374-1
ISBN-10: 1-56397-374-X
1. Thanksgiving Day—Juvenile literature. 2. Handicraft—Juvenile literature.
[1. Thanksgiving Day. 2. Handicraft.]
I. Umnik, Sharon Dunn. II. Title.
745.59—dc20   1996   CIP
Library of Congress Catalog Card Number 95-80773

First edition
Book designed by Charlie Cary
The text of this book is set in 11-point New Century Schoolbook.

10 9 8 7

Craft Contributors: Patricia Barley, Laura G. Beer, B.J. Benish, Beverly Blasucci, Linda Bloomgren,
Judy Burke, Norma Jean Byrkett, G.L. Carty, Jeanne Corrigan, Linda Douglas, Linda Faulkner,
Virginia Follis, Sandra Godfrey, Mavis Grant, Paula Hamilton, Edna Harrington, Amanda Hepburn,
Olive Howie, Garnett Kooker, Chris R. Kueng, Twilla Lamm, Lee Lindeman, Agnes Maddy, John McDowell,
June Rose Mobly, Betsy Ochester, Joan O'Donnell, Helen M. Pedersen, James W. Perrin Jr., Luella Pierce,
Louise Poe, Simone Quick, Linda Rindock, Kathy Ross, Helen R. Sattler, Karen Bornemann Spies, June
Swanson, Beth Tobler, Sharon Dunn Umnik, Jean White, Janine M. Williams, and Rebecca D. Zurawski.

Table Dress-ups

Add a festive touch to your Thanksgiving table with these apple harvest decorations.

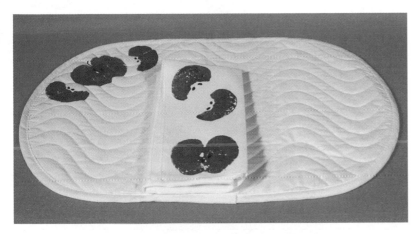

PLACE MAT AND NAPKIN
(old newspaper, apple, table knife, fabric paint, paper plate, white fabric place mat and napkin)

1. Cover your work surface with old newspaper. Cut an apple in half using a table knife. Then cut one half into quarters.

2. Squeeze some fabric paint onto a paper plate. Brush paint on one side of a quarter piece of apple or on an apple half.

3. Press the painted side of the apple section on a white fabric place mat and napkin, creating a decorative print.

4. Wash your brush. Follow the directions on the fabric-paint label for drying.

CENTERPIECE
(two apples, two candles, plastic lids, table knife)

1. *Ask an adult to help you* cut a hole from the center of two apples, large enough to hold a candle.

2. Cut feathers from different-colored plastic lids. Use a table knife to cut small slits in the apples, and insert the feathers to create a tail.

3. For each apple, draw and cut out a neck, head, and wattle from a plastic lid. Add features. Cut slits and insert the heads.

4. Place the turkeys in the center of your holiday table.

NAPKIN RING
(cardboard tube, tempera paint, poster board)

1. To make the ring, cut a 1-inch section from a cardboard tube. Paint it to look like tree bark.

2. Draw and cut out an apple from red poster board. Add a green leaf. Glue the apple to the ring and let dry.

3. Place a napkin through the ring.

HARVEST WREATH
(sixteen ice-cream sticks, watercolors, construction paper, string)

1. Paint sixteen ice-cream sticks with brown watercolor. Let dry. Glue the sticks together in pairs to form X shapes.

2. Arrange the Xs in a wreath shape and glue them together, end to end.

3. Glue a cut-paper bow, fruit, and vegetables to the wreath.

4. Tie a piece of string on the back of the wreath as a hanger.

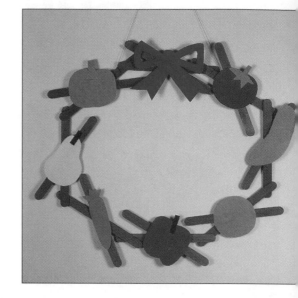

THANKSGIVING CARD
(poster board)

1. Fold a piece of poster board in half. Place your hand on the board with the longest finger touching the fold.

2. Trace around your hand with a pencil. Leaving the connection at the longest finger, cut out the hand shape.

3. Write a holiday message on the inside or the front of the hand. Stand the card up.

PUMPKIN PIE GAME
(paper plate, one die, paper, pencil)

1. Color a paper plate to look like a pumpkin pie. Cut the pie into six equal pieces, and number each piece from one through six.

To play: The first player throws the die three times. After each throw, the player removes the numbered piece of pie that matches the number on the die. Add the numbers of the pieces removed, and write the total on a score sheet. If the player rolls a duplicate number, the turn is over and the player gets no points in that round.

   After each player's turn, put the pie back together. The player with the highest score after four rounds is the winner.

RING TURKEY
(cardboard tubes, poster paint, construction paper)

1. Cut seven rings from a cardboard tube, each about 1/2 inch wide, to make the feet and tail feathers.

2. Cut another section about 2 1/2 inches wide for the body and one about 1 inch wide for the head.

3. Paint the cardboard sections. Glue them together, as shown. Cut eyes, a beak, and a wattle from construction paper. Glue them onto the turkey.

FEEDING STATION FOR BIRDS
(one-liter plastic beverage bottle, pencil, paper, bird seed, string)

1. On each side of the bottom plastic section of a one-liter plastic beverage bottle, cut a tab about 1 inch wide with scissors. Bend down the tabs, and using a paper punch, make a hole in the center of each one. Push a pencil through the holes for a perch.

2. To make the feeding holes, press a crease along each side of the bottle above the two ends of the pencil perch. Hold the crease in place, and punch a hole on the crease about 2 or 3 inches above the perch.

3. Roll a piece of paper into a cone shape, and place it in the top of the bottle to use as a funnel. Add seeds to the bottle and cap it tightly.

4. Knot string several times around the lip of the bottle just below the cap. Tie the feeder to a tree branch.

LEAF DISH
(white paper, plastic bowl, paint, permanent marker, floor wax, soft cloth)

1. Draw and cut out a large leaf shape from white paper. Trace around it, making three more leaves, all the same size. Glue all four leaves on top of one another, with the edges touching.

2. While the glue is still damp, center the leaf over an upside-down plastic bowl. Gently press the sides around the bowl to form a shallow dish. Let dry.

3. Paint the dish in fall colors. Draw dark veins, as shown, with a permanent marker.

4. *Ask an adult to help you* rub a thin coat of floor wax on the dish to make it shine. Polish with a soft cloth.

TURKEY NAPKIN HOLDER
(half-gallon milk carton, construction paper)

1. Cut off the top, bottom, and one side of an empty half-gallon milk carton. Glue brown construction paper to the outside of the carton. Then staple a strip of paper to each open end.

2. Cut out the turkey's head and feathers from colorful paper. Glue them in place on one side of the holder. Use a marker to add details to the face.

3. Place napkins inside the holder.

PILGRIM BOY AND GIRL
(construction paper, yarn)

1. To make the boy, cut three large strips from construction paper for his body. Cut a circle for his head, and glue it to the top of the body. Add hands, boots, collar, hat, and buttons made from paper. Cut pieces of yarn for hair and glue them to his head. Draw facial features with markers.

2. To make the girl, cut a large triangle from paper for her body. Cut a circle for her head, and glue it to the top of the body. Add arms, hands, boots, hat, and a bib-apron from paper. Draw facial features with markers.

3. Attach a yarn hanger to the back of the girl and the boy.

PARCHMENT PAPER
(bowl, warm tap water, two tea bags, white paper, paper towels, ribbon)

1. Add warm tap water to a bowl. Place two tea bags in the water until it has turned a dark color, then remove the bags.

2. Gently crumple a piece of white paper. Place it in the bowl, using a spoon to hold it down in the tea-colored water. Let the paper soak about fifteen minutes until it becomes a light brown color.

3. Carefully pour the water in a sink and remove the paper, letting the water drip off. Place the paper on paper towels and let it dry thoroughly. The color should vary throughout the paper when dry.

4. Write your message on the paper. Then roll it up, and tie it with ribbon.

NUTTY NOTEPAD
(tan and brown paper, cardboard, white paper)

1. Glue tan paper onto a piece of cardboard, and cut it to measure 5 inches square.

2. Draw an acorn shape on the square with a pencil, and cut it out. Draw and cut out an acorn-cap shape from brown paper, and glue it to the acorn. Add lines to the acorn cap with a marker.

3. Cut ten or more 3-inch squares of white paper to fit onto the acorn shape. Stack the papers together, put them in the center of the acorn, and staple in place.

AN AUTUMN DISPLAY
(round cardboard container, paper, old magazine, dried flowers and weeds)

1. Spread glue on the outside of a round cardboard container, such as one that holds oatmeal, and cover with paper.

2. Turn the bottom right-side up. Decorate the container with a picture cut from an old magazine.

3. Poke small holes in the bottom, and place dried flowers or dried weeds into the holes.

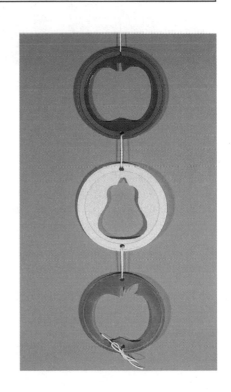

FRUIT WALL HANGING
(plastic lids, string)

1. Draw apple and pear shapes on different-colored plastic lids. Bend the lids slightly in half and carefully cut out the fruit shapes.

2. Punch a hole in each lid above and below the shape. Tie the lids together with pieces of string.

3. Attach a long string at the top for a hanger. Tie a string bow in the bottom hole of the last fruit shape. Hang the decoration on a wall.

TISSUE TURKEY

(paper plate, construction paper, tissue paper, yarn)

1. Cut out the center of a 9-inch paper plate, leaving a 2-inch rim. Turn the rim over so the bottom faces up.

2. Draw and cut out a turkey's head and feet from construction paper. Glue these to the rim.

3. To make the tail section, cut round pieces of different-colored tissue paper and glue them onto the rim.

4. Punch a hole in the rim, thread a piece of yarn through it, and tie a knot to form a hanger.

LEATHER-LIKE JOURNAL

(cardboard, masking tape, soft cloth, brown shoe polish, paper, leather shoelace)

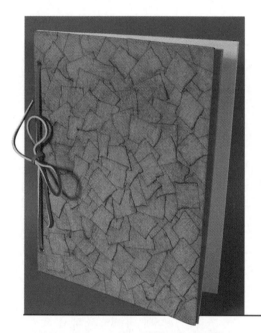

1. To make the front and back of the journal, cover both sides of two 8 1/2-by-11-inch pieces of cardboard with small torn pieces of masking tape. Using a soft cloth, rub brown shoe polish over the masking tape, giving it a rough, leather-like look.

2. With a paper punch, punch two holes in each cover, as shown. Punch holes in several 8 1/2-by-11-inch pieces of paper, making sure all the holes line up.

3. Place the sheets of paper between the covers. Thread a leather shoelace through the holes and tie a bow.

4. Make an entry every day in your journal. Add more sheets of paper as you need them.

FRUIT BOWL

(round cardboard container, construction paper, cardboard-box lid, paper doily)

1. To make the bowl, cut a round cardboard container in half lengthwise, including the lid and bottom. Cover the container with glue and construction paper.

2. To make the base, cover a cardboard-box lid with construction paper.

3. Decorate the bowl and base with pieces from a paper doily. Glue the bowl and base together and let dry. Fill the bowl with fruit, and set it in the middle of your table.

EGG-CARTON HEADS
(cardboard egg carton, poster paint, construction paper, yarn)

1. Cut the cups from a cardboard egg carton. Glue two together to make each head. Glue another to the bottom for the shoulders. Paint them and let dry.

2. Cut facial features from construction paper, and glue in place. Add a yarn bow and a white paper shirt.

3. Glue on yarn hair. Cut hats from other parts of the carton. Paint them and attach with glue.

FABRIC-LEAF MOBILE
(fabric, poster board, string, fallen tree branch)

1. Glue different colorful fabrics to both sides of white poster board. Let dry.

2. Draw and cut out leaf shapes from the different fabrics. Use a paper punch to punch a small hole in each leaf. Tie a string through each hole.

3. Tie the other ends of the strings to a small fallen tree branch. Attach another string to the center and hang the mobile where the leaves will catch the breeze and flutter.

MILK CARTON COW
(one-pint milk carton, white glue, water, bowl, paper towels, four ice-cream sticks, paper)

1. Close the top of a one-pint milk carton. Secure with staples.

2. Mix an equal amount of white glue and water in a bowl. Brush some of the mixture on the carton. Press on pieces of paper towel, adding more mixture to the pieces with a brush. Cover the entire carton and let dry.

3. Cut four slits in the carton and glue one ice-cream stick in each for a leg. Let dry.

4. Paint the body and the legs. Draw and cut out horns, ears, eyes, a nose, and a tongue from paper. Color with markers and glue in place. Add a paper tail and udders.

TURKEY NUT CUP
(plastic cup, felt, ice-cream stick, rubber band, nuts)

1. Use a plastic cup for the body of the turkey. Cut wings and tail feathers from different-colored pieces of felt. Glue them on the outside of the cup.

2. Cut one piece of felt for the neck and head. Add eyes, a beak, and wattle from felt.

3. Glue an ice-cream stick to the back of the head. Then glue the stick to the outside of the cup. Hold in place with a rubber band until dry.

4. Fill the cup with nuts.

CLAM-SHELL PLANTER
(half-gallon milk carton, construction paper, clam shells)

1. Measure up about 5 inches from the bottom of a half-gallon milk carton. Cut off the top and discard it.

2. Cover the carton with glue and construction paper.

3. Glue clean clam-shell halves in a decorative design onto one side of the carton. Let dry before adding shells to another side.

4. Place a plant inside the planter.

THE MAYFLOWER
(paper plate, paper)

1. Fold a paper plate in half so the bottom is facing you. Open the plate and draw waves with a marker on the bottom half.

2. On a piece of paper, draw a ship to represent the Mayflower. Cut it out. Fold the plate and glue the Mayflower along the top of the fold. Let dry.

3. Gently push on one end of the fold, and watch the Mayflower rock back and forth.

HAND-PAINTED TURKEY PAPER
(old newspaper, poster paper, tempera paint, paper plate)

1. Cover the floor with old newspaper. Cut a section from a roll of poster paper. Hold it in place on the newspaper with small pieces of tape in each corner.

2. Squeeze some tempera paint on a large paper plate. Place your hand in the paint until your palm and fingers are covered. Let the excess paint drip off your hand.

3. Carefully place your hand on the poster paper with your fingers spread open. Make several handprints and let dry.

4. With a black marker, add legs, a beak, and an eye to each hand, creating a turkey.

5. Use the paper to wrap holiday gifts.

STRIP PUMPKIN
(construction paper, brass fastener)

1. Cut eight strips of orange construction paper 1 inch wide and 18 inches long. Punch a hole at both ends of each strip with a paper punch.

2. Do the same with one 1-by-9-inch strip and fold it in half. This will be the stem.

3. Place the eight long strips on top of each other, as shown in the diagram. Staple in the center. Bring the ends together so the strips form a pumpkin shape. Place the stem on top. Hold everything together with a brass fastener, running through all the holes.

4. Cut and glue green paper leaves around the stem.

OAK-LEAF PIN
(poster board, felt, safety pin, acorns)

1. Draw and cut out an oak leaf from poster board to use as a pattern. Place the pattern on a piece of felt. Trace around it with a marker and cut it out. Glue the felt leaf on top of the pattern.

2. Glue an opened safety pin to the back of the leaf. Then glue a small strip of felt across the opened pin and let it dry.

3. Place three acorns on top of the leaf and attach with glue. Let dry for a day.

HOLIDAY GIFT BOX
(paint, small cardboard box, pumpkin seeds, clear nail polish)

1. Paint the outside of a small cardboard box and lid.

2. Glue pumpkin seeds in a decorative design on top of the lid. Let dry.

3. Cover the pumpkin seeds with a coat of clear nail polish to give them a glossy look.

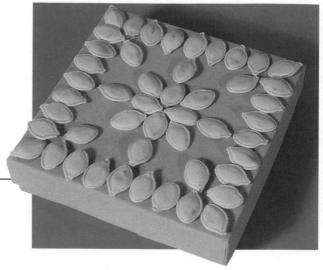

PINECONE TURKEY
(pinecone, paper plate, poster board, kernel corn)

1. Glue a pinecone to the center of a paper plate.

2. Draw and cut out colorful tail feathers and a head with a wattle and a neck from poster board. Glue the tail feathers to the flat end of the pinecone and the head to the other end.

3. Dot glue on the plate around the turkey, and add kernels of corn.

STANDING DEER
(paper, poster board)

1. On paper, draw the front section of a deer, including the antlers, head, chest, and front legs; the body, including the tail; and the hind legs. Cut out these three sections and use as patterns.

2. Place the patterns on poster board and trace around them. Cut out the sections. Add features from cut paper and glue them in place. Add other details with a marker.

3. Cut slits, as shown. Slide the legs onto the body section. You may need to adjust the slits to balance the deer.

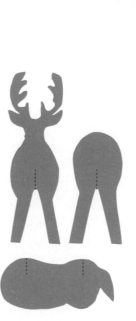

APPLE HOT PAD
(corrugated cardboard, rubber bands, paint, poster board)

1. Cut several long strips of corrugated cardboard, about 1 inch wide. Put glue on one side of a strip and wind it tightly into a coil.

2. Keep winding strips around the coil until the hot pad is as large as you would like it. Hold the strips in place with rubber bands and let dry.

3. Cover the hot pad with paint and let dry. Cut a stem and leaf from poster board. Glue them to the back of the hot pad.

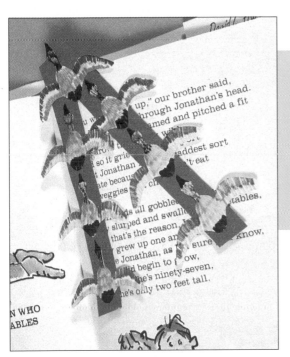

GEESE BOOKMARK
(construction paper)

1. Cut a V shape from a piece of construction paper for the base of the bookmark.

2. Draw and cut out geese from white paper. Color them with markers. Glue them along the V shape as if they were flying together.

FALL PLANTER
(cardboard food container, felt, sand, dried grasses and flowers)

1. Use a clean cardboard food container such as one in which peanuts are packaged. Measure the container and cut a piece of felt to fit around it. Glue the felt in place.

2. Cut out leaves from different-colored pieces of felt. Glue them onto the outside of the container. Add felt acorns.

3. Fill the container with sand. Arrange dried grasses and flowers in the container.

FRUIT-BOWL PICTURE
(construction paper, poster board, string)

1. Cut different colors of construction paper into long strips about 1/2 inch wide.

2. Bend and curl the strips to form shapes of a bowl and fruit. Glue the shapes onto poster board. Add strips for leaves. Let dry.

3. Cut around your design to make an attractive shape. Glue this onto poster board of a contrasting color.

4. Attach a string to the back for a hanger.

HARVEST BASKET
(construction paper, cardboard, twine, paper towels)

1. Glue construction paper on top of a sheet of cardboard. Draw a basket design on the paper with a pencil.

2. Cut and soak a piece of long twine in warm water so it will be easy to work with. Remove the twine from the water, and dry it with a paper towel. Squeeze glue on the outline of the basket, and press the twine into it.

3. Spread glue on the inside of the basket. Cut some dry twine into tiny pieces, and press them into the glue. Glue short pieces of twine in a crisscross design on top.

4. Cut fruit shapes from construction paper, and glue them at the top of the basket. Add a loop of twine to the back for a hanger.

PILGRIM CARD
(construction paper)

1. Fold a sheet of construction paper to form a card.

2. Draw a Pilgrim boy's face on another piece of paper, and cut it out. Glue it to the inside of the card, centering it on the fold.

3. Cut the top of a hat from black paper. For the brim, cut a small strip of black paper and make accordion pleats along the strip.

4. Glue the top of the hat to the card, centering on the fold. Glue one end of the accordion-pleated brim to each side of the fold.

5. Write "Happy" on the front of the card and "Thanksgiving" on the inside.

HARVEST PHOTO FRAME

(four tongue depressors, poster board, yarn, photograph)

1. Glue four tongue depressors together to form a square frame. Let dry.

2. Decorate the front of the frame by creating two ears of corn from yellow and green poster board. Add details with a black marker. Glue the corn to opposite sides of the frame.

3. Cut a piece of poster board to cover the open section of the frame. Glue it to the back. Cut and glue a yarn loop for a hanger.

4. Select a photograph. Trim if necessary and glue it onto the front.

WREATH

(heavy paper plate, large brown paper bag, construction paper, yarn)

1. To make the wreath base, cut a 7-inch circle from the center of a 10-inch heavy paper plate. Discard the circle.

2. Cut along one side and around the bottom of a large brown paper bag to make a large sheet of paper. Cut paper strips 3 inches wide.

3. Glue one end of a paper strip to the wreath base. Wrap the strip around the base, glue the end, and continue with another strip until the base is covered.

4. Cut leaves and acorns from construction paper. Add veins with a marker. Glue the paper cutouts to the wreath. Add a yarn hanger to the back.

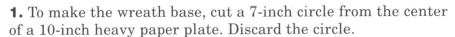

TURKEY TREAT HOLDER

(plastic bottle, construction paper)

1. For the holder, cut a 3-inch bottom section from a plastic bottle. Discard the top.

2. Draw and cut out a head, feet, and wings from construction paper. Add cut-paper features to the head. Glue the head, feet, and wings to the holder.

3. To make the tail, draw a fan shape on colored paper and cut it out. Glue this to another sheet of colored paper. Trim away the extra paper, leaving a border. Continue to do this until the tail has as many colors as you want. Glue the tail in place.

4. Fill the holder with treats.

FALL PLACE MAT

(construction paper, tempera paint, paper towels, fallen leaves, clear self-adhesive paper)

1. Under a sink faucet, wet one side of a large sheet of white construction paper. Using paintbrushes, drop yellow, green, and red tempera paint here and there onto the wet paper.

2. Tip the paper back and forth over the sink until the colors run across the paper. Let the paper dry on a bed of paper towels.

3. On a black sheet of paper, trace around a variety of fallen leaves. Carefully poke your scissors into each leaf shape and cut it out.

4. Glue the black paper over the painted paper to see the autumn leaves. *Ask an adult to help you* cover your place mat with clear self-adhesive paper.

BOX TURKEY

(two gelatin boxes, toothpaste boxes, construction paper)

1. To make the turkey's body, tape two gelatin boxes together. To make the feet and the head, cut sections from toothpaste boxes. Cover the boxes with construction paper and glue them together.

2. To make the tail feathers, cut feather shapes from several colors of construction paper and glue them together, as shown. Glue the tail feathers to the back of the turkey.

3. Cut wings, eyes, a beak, and a wattle from construction paper, and glue onto the turkey.

Glue tail feathers

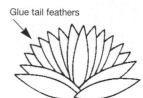

MAYFLOWER'S CROW'S NEST

(heavyweight paper, ice-cream stick, plastic-foam cup)

1. Draw and cut out a Pilgrim boy from heavyweight paper. Add features with markers. Glue the boy to one end of an ice-cream stick.

2. Push the other end of the ice-cream stick through the bottom of a plastic-foam cup so the boy is inside. Draw railings around the outside of the cup.

3. Hold the stick with one hand and the cup with the other. Make the Pilgrim boy pop up and down as he looks over the rail of the crow's nest.

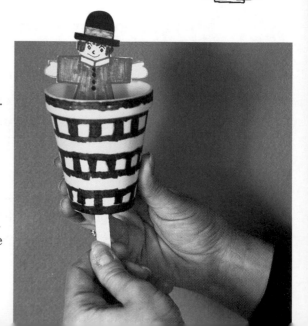

CHANCE OF FLURRIES
(paper, glitter, string)

1. Tape two sheets of paper together to form a long sheet. Starting at the short side of the paper, fold accordion pleats. Staple the folded paper in the middle.

2. Cut the two ends at an angle. Cut through all the folds to make small triangles.

3. Spread open the folds until the ends meet, forming a circle. Tape the ends together.

4. Add dabs of glue and sprinkle with glitter. Let dry. Glue a piece of string for a hanger.

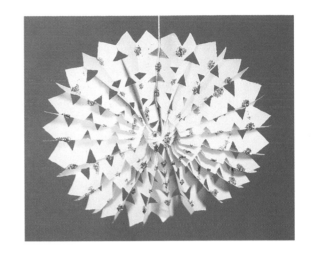

STUFF-THE-TURKEY GAME
(one large brown paper bag, two small brown paper bags, old newspaper, tissue paper)

1. Fold down 4 inches of a large brown paper bag, keeping the fold inside. Gather the corner edges together so the opening of the bag is a little smaller, and staple in place. Push out the corners to round out the body of the "turkey."

2. Stuff two small brown paper bags with old newspaper. Twist the bags to form "drumsticks." Cut strips of red tissue paper and glue around the ends to make frills. Glue the "drumsticks" to opposite sides of the body.

3. For "bread stuffing," wad up sheets of newspaper. Cover them with white tissue paper and hold together with pieces of tape.

To play: Players take turns tossing the "stuffing" into the "turkey" from a distance of four to five feet. See who can get the most "stuffing" into the "turkey."

MILKWEED-POD MOUSE
(milkweed-pod half, construction paper, moveable plastic eyes, sewing needle, black thread)

1. Select a dried milkweed-pod half with a stem, which will be used as a tail for the mouse.

2. Cut two ears, two eyes, and a nose from construction paper and glue in place. Glue moveable plastic eyes on top of the paper eyes.

3. Thread a sewing needle with black thread. Carefully poke the needle and thread through the nose area of the milkweed pod. When through, cut the thread to look like a whisker. Do this several times.

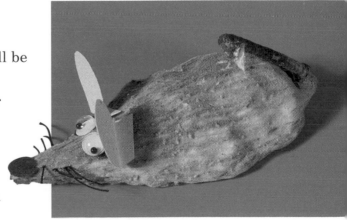

CORNUCOPIA

(old T-shirts or socks, needle and thread, cotton, felt, yarn, paper plate)

1. Using old T-shirts or socks, cut long, narrow, and wide rectangles to make different vegetables and fruits.

2. Fold each rectangle in half. With a needle and thread, sew up all but one short side. Turn the shape inside out, and stuff with cotton.

3. Sew up the fourth side, and add leaves made of felt or yarn.

4. Roll a paper plate into the shape of a cornucopia, and staple the ends together. Place the fruits and vegetables inside.

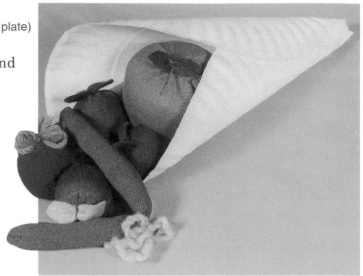

DOORKNOB TURKEY

(construction paper, yarn)

1. Draw and cut out a turkey shape from construction paper. Color the turkey with crayons, as shown.

2. Punch two holes in the tail area, and tie a loop of yarn for a hanger.

3. Place the turkey on a doorknob in your home.

PILGRIM BOOKENDS

(two half-gallon milk cartons, construction paper, rocks)

1. Cut two half-gallon milk cartons in half and discard the tops. Glue construction paper around each carton.

2. Draw and cut out a Pilgrim boy and Pilgrim girl from paper. Glue them to one side of a carton.

3. Place rocks inside the cartons so they will be heavy enough to hold books in place.

PUMPKIN CRUMBER
(two heavy paper plates, poster paint, ribbon)

1. Cut a heavy paper plate in half. Cover it with orange poster paint and let dry.

2. Cut a stem and leaf from another heavy paper plate. Paint them and let dry. Glue the stem and leaf to one plate half so when the other half is joined it looks like a pumpkin.

3. Glue a piece of orange ribbon along the bottom of the pumpkin's top half. Let this dry.

4. Gently sweep the top half of the pumpkin over your holiday tablecloth, brushing the crumbs from the table into the bottom half of the pumpkin. Discard the crumbs.

APPLE WALL HANGING
(felt, three brass fasteners, three plastic lids, paper, metal ring)

1. Cut a strip of felt 3 by 30 inches. Cut each end to a point. Push a brass fastener through the center of each of the plastic lids. Attach the lids to the felt strip.

2. Draw pictures on round pieces of paper, and glue them to the centers of the lids. Glue a metal ring at the top for hanging.

LEAF NAPKIN RING
(paper, felt, permanent marker)

1. To make a pattern, draw and cut out an oak leaf shape from paper, as shown.

2. Pin the paper leaf on felt and cut around the pattern. Do this twice, using two different-colored pieces of felt. Draw veins on the leaves with a permanent marker.

3. Glue the stems of the leaves together. Cut a slit in one leaf just above the stem. Pull the uncut leaf through the slit, forming a ring with the stems.

4. Place a napkin in the ring.

LEAF-TURKEY PICTURE
(paper, fallen leaves)

1. Cut the body of the turkey from a piece of paper. Glue it onto another piece of paper.

2. Collect different kinds of fallen leaves for the tail feathers. Glue the leaves in place.

3. Add features with pieces of cut paper and attach with glue.

SQUIRREL NUT BOX
(fabric, small jewelry box, acorns)

1. Cut and glue small strips of fabric around the lid and the bottom of a small jewelry box.

2. Place four acorns in the center of the lid and attach with glue. Let dry for about a day.

3. Store little keepsakes in the box.

PAPER CHAIN
(construction paper)

1. Cut strips of construction paper measuring 3 by 18 inches. Fold over 3 inches of one strip at one end, making a 3-inch square. Continue to fold into accordion pleats until the whole strip is pleated.

2. On the top square, draw a pumpkin shape with the edges touching the folds.

3. Keeping the strip folded, cut out the pumpkin. Do not cut through the folded paper at the edges. Unfold the paper. Use five pumpkins and write one letter of the word "Happy" on each pumpkin.

4. To create the word "Thanksgiving," follow steps 1, 2, and 3, but tape two strips together at one end to make twelve pumpkins.

CORNFIELD BOWLING
(ten one-quart milk cartons, brown wrapping paper, construction paper, rubber ball)

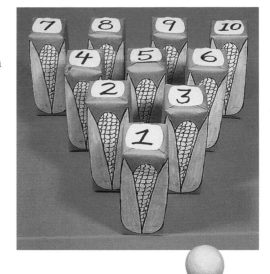

1. Fold over the tops of ten one-quart milk cartons and seal with tape. Cover each carton with brown wrapping paper.

2. Draw ten ears of corn on white construction paper and color with markers. Glue an ear of corn to one side of each milk carton.

3. Cut ten kernels of corn from yellow paper and number them 1 through 10. Glue a kernel to the top of each milk carton.

To play: Set up the ten ears of corn like pins in bowling. Using a rubber ball, bowl over as many ears as you can and total the number of points scored. Each player gets one turn. The player with the highest score wins.

FINGERPRINT STATIONERY
(paper, tempera paint)

1. Select paper for your stationery.

2. Using tempera paint, brush a small amount of paint on your fingertip. Practice making fingerprints on a piece of scrap paper.

3. Make fingerprints in various places on the stationery. With markers, add feathers, eyes, a beak, and feet to each fingerprint, making little turkeys.

FALL BANNER
(felt, fabric glue, wooden dowel, decorative trim)

1. Lay four pieces of felt vertically, overlapping the edges about 1 inch. Glue them together with fabric glue.

2. Fold the top edge of the first piece of felt over a small wooden dowel and hold in place with glue. Let dry.

3. Cut fall symbols such as leaves, a turkey, a pumpkin, and corn from pieces of felt and glue onto the panels.

4. Glue or staple decorative trim around the ends of the wooden dowel for a hanger.

BEAN NECKLACE

(plastic lid, dried beans and lentils, ribbon)

1. Spread glue around the inside of a plastic lid. Place a variety of dried beans and lentils in the glue, making a decorative design. Let dry.

2. Cut a long piece of ribbon. Glue the ribbon around the outside rim of the lid, leaving two equal ends of ribbon to tie around your neck.

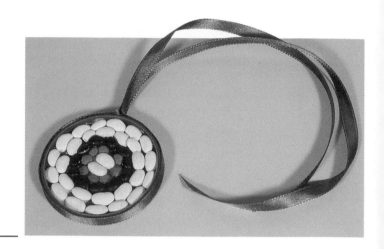

BASKET OF GOURDS

(cardboard, felt, wicker basket, ornamental gourds)

1. Draw and cut out different types of leaves from cardboard to use as patterns. Trace around the patterns on felt. Cut out the leaves.

2. Glue the leaves on the outside of a wicker basket and let dry.

3. Place a variety of ornamental gourds in the basket. Set the basket in the center of a table.

GRANDPARENT HOLIDAY CARD

(poster board, felt, photographs)

1. Cut a rectangle from a piece of white poster board. Draw and cut out a cornucopia from a piece of brightly colored felt.

2. Glue the cornucopia on the poster board. At the opening of the cornucopia, glue photographs of your family.

3. Write a message such as "Happy Thanksgiving to Grandma and Grandpa from all of us!"

TURKEY PLACE CARD
(two tongue depressors, construction paper, one toothpick, cotton ball, corn kernels)

1. Glue the bottom edge of one tongue depressor to the back edge of another tongue depressor. Let dry. Cut a small piece of construction paper and write a guest's name on it. Glue it on a tongue depressor, as shown.

2. Color a toothpick with a marker, and break it in half for the turkey's legs and feet. Glue the toothpicks into a cotton ball. Cut and glue paper tail feathers and a head onto the cotton ball. Add a wattle to the head.

3. Attach the turkey to the tongue depressor by gluing the legs in place. Glue a few corn kernels onto the flat tongue depressor.

4. Make a place card for each dinner guest.

THANKSGIVING PICTURE PUZZLE
(paper, poster board, markers)

1. Draw a holiday picture on a piece of paper using markers.

2. Glue the picture on a piece of poster board that is a little larger than the picture. Let dry.

3. Turn the picture over and lightly draw lines to create puzzle pieces. Cut along the lines.

PENCIL PILGRIMS
(paper, markers, pencils)

1. Draw a Pilgrim boy and a Pilgrim girl on a piece of paper, making sure they will be large enough to go around the top of a pencil, as shown. Cut out the shapes.

2. Trace around the boy and girl on a piece of paper, making a front and a back for each. Cut out the shapes and color with markers.

3. With a pencil in the middle, glue a front and a back shape together for each Pilgrim.

PLYMOUTH ROCK DOORSTOP
(stones, cereal box, construction paper)

1. Put some clean stones inside a cereal box for weight. Tape the flaps closed. Cover the cereal box with construction paper.

2. Draw and cut out a rock to represent the famous Plymouth Rock. Glue the rock to one side of the cereal box. Add a sign.

3. Place the doorstop by a door.

THANKSGIVING CENTERPIECE
(old newspaper, large brown paper bag, string, thin cardboard)

1. Crumple sheets of old newspaper into balls and place them in a large brown paper bag until full. Tie the top closed with string.

2. Draw a turkey head, tail, wings, and feet on thin cardboard. Cut them out and color with markers or crayons.

3. Flatten the top of the bag and glue the head in place. Glue on the tail, wings, and feet.

VASE OF CHRYSANTHEMUMS
(construction paper)

1. Use a 12-by-18-inch piece of construction paper for the background. Cut out and glue on a vase from paper.

2. Cut circles measuring 7, 5 1/2, 4 1/2, and 2 1/2 inches for each flower. Cut slits around the outer edges to make fringes. Curl the fringes around a pencil.

3. Glue the largest fringed circle to the construction paper, then add the other circles. End with the smallest in the center. Add paper stems and leaves.

AUTUMN GREETING
(pear, tempera paint, paper)

1. *Ask an adult to help you* cut a pear in half. Paint the cut side of the pear with tempera paint. Press it onto a sheet of white paper. Let the print dry.

2. Fold a piece of colored paper in half to make a card. Glue the white-paper print onto the front of the card.

3. Write a message inside.

PIGGY MAGNET
(frozen-juice pull-top lid, construction paper, buttons, moveable plastic eyes, chenille stick, magnetic strip)

1. Trace around a frozen-juice pull-top lid on a piece of pink construction paper. Cut out the circle and glue it to the lid.

2. Glue a large button nose to the center of the lid. Add a smaller button in the center of the larger one. Add moveable plastic eyes, button ears, and button feet.

3. Cut a small piece from a chenille stick, curl it around a pencil, and glue it to the back of the lid for the tail.

4. Glue a small magnetic strip to the back of the lid.

FEED THE TURKEY
(large cardboard box, brown wrapping paper, construction paper, poster board, fabric, dried beans, rubber bands)

1. Remove the flaps from one end of a large cardboard box. Cover the rest of the box with brown wrapping paper, leaving the open end uncovered. Place the box on your work surface with the opened end as the bottom.

2. Make eyes, eyelashes, and a large beak from construction paper. Glue them onto the front of the box. Cut tail feathers from poster board, and tape them onto the back of the box.

3. *Ask an adult to help you* cut a large hole under the beak.

4. To make large kernels of corn, cut out three circles about 7 inches in diameter from yellow fabric. Place dried beans in the center of each circle and gather the edges. Hold together with rubber bands.

5. See who can toss the most kernels into the turkey's mouth.

PAPER ACORN WREATH

(paper plate, brown wrapping paper, gold wrapping paper, ribbon, yarn)

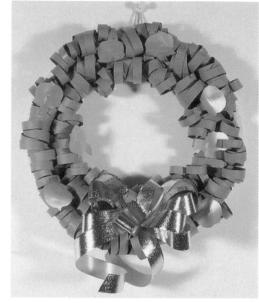

1. Cut the center from a paper plate. Use the outer ring as the base for the wreath.

2. Cut a piece of brown wrapping paper about 7 by 3 inches. Leaving about 1 inch in the center uncut, cut slits in both short ends of the strip to make fringes. Curl the fringes around a pencil. Glue this to the wreath base. Make more sections until the wreath is filled.

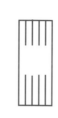

3. To decorate, draw and cut out acorn shapes from gold wrapping paper. Glue them around the wreath. Add a ribbon.

4. Glue a yarn loop to the back for a hanger.

PILGRIM HOUSE

(paper, construction paper, yarn)

1. Draw a Pilgrim house on a piece of paper with markers or crayons. Trim around the picture.

2. Place the picture on a large piece of construction paper. Punch a hole in the middle of the picture near the top, and tie a loop of yarn for a hanger.

TUBE TURKEY

(bathroom tissue tube, tempera paint)

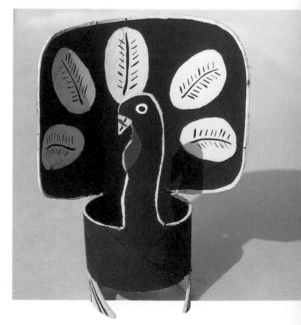

1. Cut sections from one end of a bathroom tissue tube for feet, as shown.

2. At the front of the turkey, cut two 3-inch slits, about 1 inch apart, starting at the top of the tube. Trim this 1-inch section, making the turkey's neck and head. Cut the tube near the base of the neck, as shown, to form the tail. Round the corners.

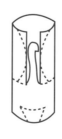

3. Decorate with tempera paint.

FRUIT COASTERS
(felt, plastic lids)

1. Cut circles of felt and glue them on the insides of plastic lids.

2. Draw and cut out fruit shapes, such as apples or pears. Glue them on top of the felt

GIFT BAG
(brown paper bag, construction paper, ribbon)

1. Fold over the top flap of a brown paper bag about 3 inches. Cut pieces of construction paper to make a Pilgrim girl's head, including the collar. Glue onto the bag.

2. With the bag folded, punch a hole on each side of the collar and through the layers of the bag. Thread a piece of ribbon through the holes and tie a bow. This will hold the bag closed.

3. Decorate the rest of the bag with paper, making the girl's hands, dress, and apron.

CLOTHING TRUNK
(shoe box, brown wrapping paper, ribbon,
gold wrapping paper)

1. Cover a shoe box and lid separately with brown wrapping paper.

2. Cut and glue pieces of ribbon as strapping around the box. Do the same with the lid, matching the strapping on the box.

3. To make hinges in the back, cut two pieces of ribbon. With the lid on the box, glue each piece of ribbon over the strapping, connecting the lid and the box together. Let dry.

4. Add a decorative latch cut from gold wrapping paper. Glue diamond shapes to the hinges.

WHEAT BOOKMARK
(poster board, broomstraw)

1. Draw and cut out a wheat shape from poster board. Decorate with markers.

2. Glue pieces of broomstraw to the back of the bookmark.

TURKEY TISSUE BOX
(box of facial tissues, brown wrapping paper, construction paper)

1. Cover a box of facial tissues on three sides with brown wrapping paper. On the fourth side, cover the box only up to the slot through which the facial tissues will be removed.

2. Cut tail feathers from construction paper, and tape them around the slot.

3. Decorate the front of the box with paper eyes, a beak, a wattle, a beard, and feet. Add paper wings to the sides of the box.

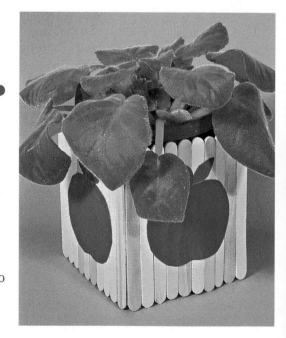

PLANTER
(half-gallon milk carton, ice-cream sticks, construction paper)

1. Cut away the top of a half-gallon milk carton so the bottom is slightly shorter than an ice-cream stick.

2. Glue ice-cream sticks on each side of the carton. Let each side dry before starting another side.

3. Cut apple shapes from construction paper, and glue them to the sides. Add paper leaves.

4. Place a potted plant inside.

RECIPE CARDS

(tempera paint, paper plate, plain index cards)

1. Squeeze drops of tempera paint onto a paper plate. Dip a fingertip in one color and press it in a corner of an index card.

2. Clean your fingertip before using a different color on another card.

3. Decorate the fingerprints with markers, creating holiday figures or scenes.

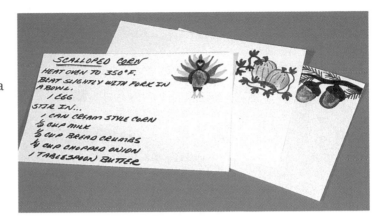

APPLE MOBILE

(two tongue depressors, felt, five frozen-juice pull-top lids, yarn)

1. Glue two tongue depressors in the shape of an X and let dry.

2. Draw and cut out two apple shapes from red felt for each juice lid. Cut a green stem and leaf for each apple.

3. Cut lengths of green yarn. Glue the end of a piece of yarn on one side of a lid. Add a felt apple on top. Glue a felt apple on the other side of the lid. Add a stem and a leaf to each apple. Let dry. Do this for each apple.

4. Tie one apple to the center of the X. Tie the other four apples to the ends of the tongue depressors. Add glue to the tied ends. Tie yarn in the center to hang.

WOOLLY-BEAR DRAFT STOPPER

(felt, needle and thread, old rags or cotton batting, buttons)

1. Sew two brown-felt rectangles together. Then sew a black rectangle to each end.

2. Fold the right sides together and sew along the long side using brown and black thread where needed. Stitch one end closed.

3. Reach your hand inside, grab the end, and turn the felt right-side out. Stuff with old rags or cotton batting. Sew the open end closed. Add button eyes.

4. Place the woolly bear at the bottom of a door to stop any draft from coming in.

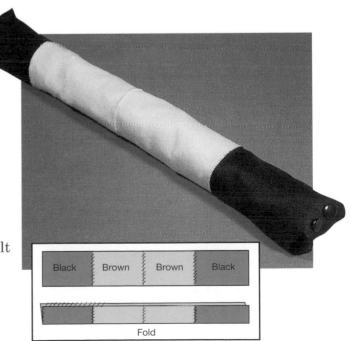

Black	Brown	Brown	Black

Fold

STRAW BRUSH
(broomstraw, fallen tree branch, rubber band, ribbon)

1. Cut pieces of broomstraw from an old broom.

2. Gather the straw around a piece of a fallen tree branch. Hold in place with a rubber band.

3. Trim the broomstraw ends evenly with scissors. Tie a ribbon on top of the rubber band.

SHAPE TURKEY
(construction paper)

1. From different colors of construction paper, cut circles about 7 inches, 6 1/2 inches, 4 inches, 2 1/2 inches, and 1 1/2 inches wide.

2. Cut feet for the turkey to match the color of the largest circle. Place the circles as shown.

3. From paper, cut out a neck and a small circle for the face. Add a beak, eyes, wattle, and beard

4. Glue the turkey to a large sheet of paper.

PAPER-BAG PILGRIM MASK
(large brown paper bag, construction paper)

1. Measure about 6 inches from the opening of a large paper bag, and cut around the entire bag.

2. Cover the front of the bag with construction paper. Put the bag on your head. Using a crayon, have a friend carefully mark where the eyeholes should be on the outside of the bag. Remove the bag.

3. Cut out the eyeholes. Cut out and glue pieces of paper to make eyebrows, a moustache, and hair.

4. To make the collar, cut a strip of white paper. Fold it in accordion pleats. Open it up and glue it in place.

5. Draw and cut out a black hat from paper. Add a brown-paper band. Glue the hat to the top of the head.

BOOKREST
(corrugated cardboard)

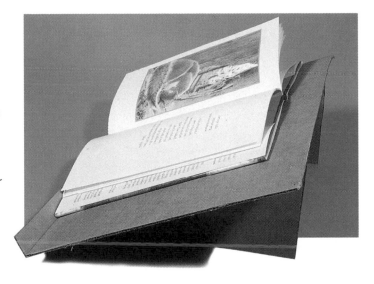

1. For the bookrest, cut a piece of corrugated cardboard to measure 12 by 18 inches.

2. Cut a strip of corrugated cardboard 1 by 18 inches for the ledge. Glue it to the bottom edge of the rest.

3. Cut two pieces of corrugated cardboard, as shown, for the stands. Glue them to the bottom of the bookrest.

4. Use markers to draw a wood-like grain on the bookrest.

SUET HOLDER FOR BIRDS
(plastic-mesh vegetable bag, suet, string, ribbon)

1. Reuse a plastic-mesh vegetable bag by filling it with suet, purchased from the supermarket, for the birds to eat.

2. Gather the opened end and tie it closed with string, wrapping the string around several times before knotting. Leave the ends of the string long so the holder can be tied to a tree limb. Add a ribbon.

3. Tie a ribbon at the bottom.

THREE-DIMENSIONAL FISH
(poster board, tissue paper, paper plate, yarn)

1. Cut a rectangular piece of poster board. Make a decorative border around the edges with a marker. Lightly sketch a fish shape in the middle.

2. Tear colored tissue paper into little pieces. Squeeze a small amount of white glue onto a paper plate.

3. Dip the pieces of tissue paper into the glue and place them inside the fish drawing, making a textured effect. Continue to fill the drawing.

4. Tape or glue a piece of yarn in the back for a hanger.

Travel Helpers

Create these playful travel accessories to make your holiday trip even more fun.

PILLOWCASE TOTE
(white pillowcase, cardboard, permanent markers or fabric paint, decorative cording)

1. Place a white pillowcase on a flat work surface. Insert a piece of cardboard inside. (This will protect the markers or paint from going through to the back of the pillowcase.)

2. With permanent markers or fabric paint, draw on pictures of clothing you might put in the tote.

3. Cut a small slit in the hem on each side of the seam near the opening of the pillowcase. Insert decorative cording in one slit, pulling the cord through the hem and out the second slit. Tie the ends of the cord together.

4. Close by pulling the cord and tightly gathering the pillowcase top.

CAN OF FUN
(cardboard container with lid, paper)

1. Cut a piece of paper the correct size to cover the outside of a tall, round cardboard container.

2. Write "Can of Fun!" in the center of the paper. Draw pictures on it. Glue the picture around the container.

3. Place pencils, pens, markers, small pieces of note paper, scissors, and tape inside.

LUGGAGE TAG
(corrugated cardboard, paper, yarn)

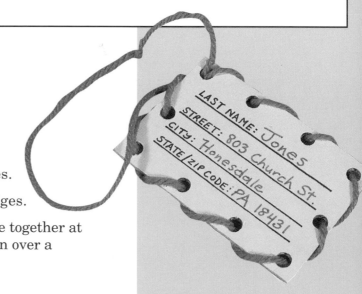

1. Cut a small rectangle from a piece of corrugated cardboard. Glue a piece of bright paper to both sides.

2. Using a paper punch, punch holes around the edges.

3. Weave a long piece of yarn through the holes and tie together at the end. To place the tag on your luggage, loop the yarn over a handle and pull the tag through the loop.

GOOD-GROOMING TRAVEL KIT
(felt, fabric place mat, fabric glue, rickrack, ribbon)

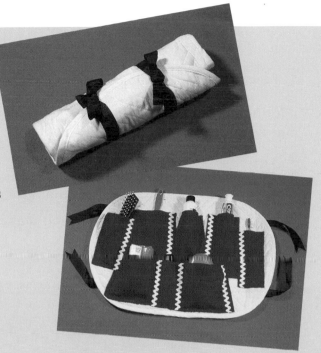

1. Cut felt squares and rectangles to hold the shapes of the items you will place in the kit, such as a brush, comb, shampoo, toothpaste, and soap. Place the pocket shapes on the place mat, making sure each item will fit its pocket. Put fabric glue on the bottom and the sides of each pocket. Press the pockets onto the place mat. Decorate with pieces of rickrack. Let dry overnight.

2. Place the toiletries in their pockets. Tightly roll up the place mat. Cut two pieces of ribbon long enough to fit around the rolled place mat. Tie the ribbons, as shown, to hold the kit together.

3. When you open the kit, place the ribbons in one of the pockets so they don't get lost.

PERSONAL PET BOX
(shoe box, paper, two plastic containers, one plastic bottle, sandwich bags)

1. Decorate the outside of a shoe box with paper cutouts of paw prints and biscuits.

2. Use two plastic containers, one for food and one for water, as feeding dishes for your pet. Extra water can be stored in a plastic bottle. Treats can be placed in a sandwich bag.

3. Store other items such as a toy and a leash.

TRAVEL ACTIVITY BOX
(cardboard candy box, brown wrapping paper, felt)

1. Cover the outside of an empty cardboard candy-box lid with brown wrapping paper. Cut and glue pieces of felt on the lid, making a scene.

2. Glue a piece of felt inside on the bottom of the box. Use this as your activity board.

3. Cut various objects from felt. Place the cutouts on the felt inside the box to create different scenes. Cut two white strips, five red circles, and five green circles from felt to play tic-tac-toe. Store the felt pieces in the box.

GLOVE TURKEY PUPPET
(brown cotton glove, felt, moveable plastic eye)

1. Place a brown cotton glove with the palm side facing up. Cut a beak, a wattle, and an eye from felt and glue onto the thumb. Add a moveable plastic eye to the felt eye.

2. Cut tail feathers from felt and glue one feather to each of the four fingers. Cut out a wing from felt and glue on the palm.

3. Insert your hand in the glove and make your turkey run.

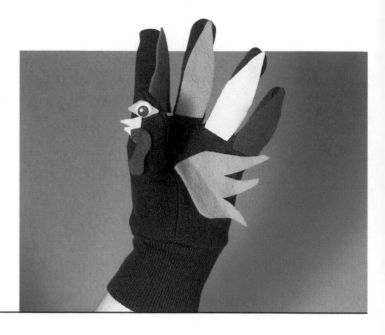

BLACK CROW
(two index cards, penny, yarn)

1. Draw a crow flying with its wings extended on one index card. Draw a crow on another index card with its wings in another flying position.

2. Glue a penny to the middle of the back of one card to add weight so it will spin.

3. Cut a 36-inch piece of yarn, double it, and knot the ends. Find the middle of the doubled yarn, and glue it to the back of one of the cards.

4. Glue the cards together with the pictures outside and with the yarn extending from the right and left sides. Wind the card by holding the ends of the yarn and spinning the card. Firmly pull the ends of the yarn away from the card and watch the crow fly.

CORN-CHIP BASKET
(fabric, plastic berry basket)

1. Cut long strips of yellow fabric wide enough to be woven in and out of sections of a plastic berry basket.

2. Weave one strip per section, as shown. Tie the ends into a bow. Fill the basket with corn chips.

PAPER-BAG PILGRIMS
(tempera paint, two small brown paper bags, old newspaper, paper)

1. For the bodies, paint two small paper bags with tempera paint and let dry. Wad up old newspaper and stuff each bag. Fold back the top corners and fold the opening back twice. Glue in place.

2. Cut out arms and shoes from paper and paint them the same color as the bodies. When dry, glue to the bodies.

3. To make a Pilgrim man and woman, draw and cut out paper heads. Add features. Draw and cut out hats and details for the clothing and glue in place.

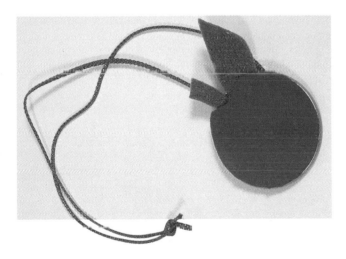

APPLE NECKLACE
(felt, frozen-juice pull-top lid, cording)

1. Draw and cut out an apple, stem, and leaf from felt. Glue them to a frozen-juice pull-top lid.

2. Cut a piece of cording long enough for a necklace. Knot the ends. Find the middle of the cording, and glue it to the back of the lid.

LITTLE WHITE CHURCH CARD
(brown paper bag, pencil)

1. Cut a piece of brown paper bag 9 by 12 inches. Fold it in half (6 by 9 inches), then fold in half again the other way (6 by 4 1/2 inches).

2. On the inside fold line, draw a church, making sure the center of the church is on the fold line. Cut through only one layer of paper along the roof and the bottom of the church, as shown. With a pencil, pull the church forward and reverse the fold.

Cut

Cut

3. Close the card, press down, and reopen. Your church now stands out.

4. Color a scene around the church.

Fold out

TURKEY-FOOT PLACE MAT
(poster board)

1. Draw and cut out the shape of a turkey footprint from a large piece of poster board.

2. Draw and cut out the talons from another piece of poster board and glue them onto the place mat.

3. Make one place mat for each guest.

PAPER-TUBE TURKEY
(paper towel tube, poster paint, brown paper bag, construction paper)

1. Cut a paper towel tube on a slant and make slices about 3/4 inch wide. Paint the slices bright colors and let them dry.

2. Cut out the turkey's body and feet from a brown paper bag, and glue them to a large sheet of construction paper.

3. For the tail feathers, glue the slices to the body with the holes facing up. Add a cut-paper beak and wattle.

WREATH OF LEAVES
(poster board, yarn, glitter, fabric)

1. Cut a doughnut shape from poster board to make the base of the wreath. Wrap yarn completely around it.

2. Draw and cut out leaves from colored poster board. Spread glue around the edges of the leaves and sprinkle them with glitter. Let dry.

3. Glue the leaves to the wreath. Cut a strip of fabric and make a bow. Tie it to the wreath. Attach a loop of yarn to the back for a hanger.

RAINBOW TURKEY
(cardboard box, construction paper, paper plate)

1. To make the body of the turkey, cover a cardboard box with construction paper.

2. To make the tail, cut a paper plate in half. Divide the front and back of one plate half into sections. Color each section with a crayon or marker. Glue the tail to the back of the box.

3. To make the wings, cut the remaining half of the paper plate in half. Divide the front and back of each half into sections. Color both sides. Glue the wings to the sides of the box.

4. Draw and cut out a head and neck from paper. Add features. Glue the shape to the front of the box.

PHOTO ALBUM
(three-ring binder, scrap wallpaper, poster board)

1. Cover a three-ring binder with scrap wallpaper.

2. Make a label from poster board and glue it to the front of the album.

WALNUT-MICE RACERS
(walnut halves, tempera paint, construction paper, moveable plastic eyes, yarn, marbles)

1. Cover two walnut halves with different-colored tempera paint and let dry.

2. Cut and glue paper ears on each walnut half. Add paper noses and moveable plastic eyes. Paint whiskers around the noses. Glue small pieces of yarn for tails.

3. Place a small marble under each mouse. Set them on a board. Tilt the board so the mice race down it.

PILGRIM PLACE CARD
(poster board)

1. Draw a Pilgrim boy from the waist up on a piece of poster board. Color with markers.

2. Cut out the boy, as shown, making a long tab. Fold at the dotted lines so he will stand.

BAKING-CUP TURKEY CAN
(paper baking cup, construction paper, round cardboard container with lid)

1. Spread open a paper baking cup. Cut the cup in half. Cut out the half-circle of one cup half and shape the pleated section into two wings.

2. Use the other half for the fan-shaped tail, cutting small slashes in it. Cut a body and feet from construction paper and color with markers. Glue all the parts in the center of a piece of paper.

3. Cover a round cardboard container with construction paper. Glue the turkey picture onto the container.

PIN THE TAIL ON THE TURKEY
(white paper, poster board, corrugated cardboard, yarn, pushpins)

1. Draw a large picture of a turkey on white paper. Cut out the drawing, and glue it in the center of a large piece of poster board.

2. Glue the poster board on a sheet of corrugated cardboard. Punch two holes, one at each corner, and tie a piece of yarn for a hanger.

3. Cut tail feathers from poster board, using a variety of colors. Press a pushpin in the base of a tail feather.

To play: Hang the turkey on a wall. All players receive a tail feather with a pushpin. Blindfold the players when it's their turn. Spin the players around, point them in the direction of the turkey, and let them pin their tail feathers on the turkey.

MILKWEED-POD BOX
(pinking shears, construction paper, white gift box, dried milkweed-pod halves, lentils)

1. Using pinking shears to give a saw-toothed design, cut a piece of construction paper to fit the top of a white gift box. Glue the paper to the top of the box.

2. Arrange a design of dried milkweed-pod halves as flower petals and lentils for the flower's center. Glue in place and let dry.

OWL GIFT BAG
(construction paper, brown paper bag, chenille stick)

1. Cut two hearts, about 6 inches square, from construction paper.

2. Cut paper wings and glue them to one of the hearts. Add paper feet. Glue the heart to the front of a brown paper bag, 1 inch down from the opening.

3. To make the head, fold down 3 inches of the second heart. Cut and glue paper eyes and a beak to the folded flap. Cut paper triangles for ear tufts and glue them under the flap, just below the fold, so they stick out at the sides.

4. Open the folded heart and spread glue below the fold. Press it against the back side of the bag so the fold is even with the top of the bag.

5. To make a handle, bend a chenille stick in a horseshoe shape, with 2 inches at each end bent toward the center. Tape the ends inside the fold.

6. Close the bag by folding the flap down. Draw curved lines on the owl to make feathers.

CORNUCOPIA WALL HANGING
(plastic-foam trays, poster board, rickrack, yarn)

1. Draw and cut out a cornucopia shape from a large plastic-foam tray. Glue it on a piece of poster board.

2. Draw and cut out various fruit and vegetable shapes from different-colored plastic-foam trays. Glue them at the opening of the cornucopia.

3. Glue a strip of rickrack across the top and bottom of the poster board. Punch two holes at the top and tie a yarn hanger.

TUBE PILGRIMS

(bathroom tissue tubes, brown paper bag, poster paint, paper)

1. Use a bathroom tissue tube for each body. To make arms, cut circles from a brown paper bag, slit to the center, shape into cones, and glue. Cut a man's hat from brown paper. Paint the body, arms, and hat with poster paint and let dry.

2. For the heads, cut two 1 1/2-inch-wide rings from a bathroom tissue tube. Paint them and let dry.

3. Glue the arms, heads, and the man's hat to the bodies. Add cut-paper features to each head. Cut out a hat and glue onto the woman. Add other paper features.

BEAN SHADOW BOX

(paper, small shallow box, dried beans and lentils, yarn)

1. Glue a piece of paper inside a small shallow box. Use dried beans and lentils to design a flower inside the box.

2. Squeeze dabs of glue on the paper and place the beans or lentils in the design.

3. Cut and glue a loop of yarn to the back of the box for a hanger.

TURKEY PAPERWEIGHT

(rock, construction paper, cardboard egg carton, poster paint)

1. Find a rock that looks like a fat turkey body. Wash and dry the rock.

2. From construction paper, cut feathers of different sizes for the tail. Cut paper wings. Glue them to the rock body.

3. Cut a cup from a cardboard egg carton and cover with poster paint. Let dry. Add paper eyes and a beak. Glue the head on the body.

HAIR CLIP
(3-inch metal barrette base, cardboard, ribbon, rubber band, poster board)

1. Recycle a metal barrette base by removing the old ribbon.

2. Cut a 3-inch-long piece of cardboard the width of your ribbon. Glue a piece of ribbon around the cardboard, securing the ends underneath it. Glue the cardboard to the top of the barrette. Hold it in place with a rubber band and let dry.

3. Glue a smaller ribbon of another color on top of the first ribbon, as shown. Draw and cut out fruit shapes from poster board. Add details with a marker. Glue them on top of the ribbon.

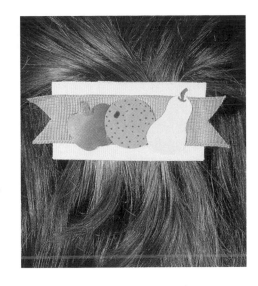

WISHBONE WELCOME
(paper, string, ribbon)

1. Cut a wishbone shape from a piece of paper. Punch a hole at the top and tie a piece of string for a hanger.

2. Punch two holes just below the hanger and tie a bow from ribbon. Punch a hole at each end of the wishbone.

3. Make a sign on a rectangular piece of paper. Write "Welcome, we wish you a happy Thanksgiving."

4. Punch a hole at the top corners of the sign to line up with the holes at the ends of the wishbone. Tie the sign to the wishbone with string.

RECIPE HOLDER
(small cardboard box, 4-by-6-inch index cards, fabric, felt)

1. With tape, close the opening of a small cardboard box, such as one that holds cookies.

2. *Ask an adult to help you* cut off one side panel. A 4-by-6-inch index card should fit inside.

3. Spread glue on the outside and 1 inch inside the box opening. Cut out a piece of fabric and press it into the glue, covering the box.

4. Cut out letters from felt to spell the word "Recipes." Glue the letters to one side of the box. Fill the box with recipes written on the index cards.

POTATO TURKEY
(potato, poster board, table knife, bathroom tissue tube)

1. Wash and dry a potato that looks like a fat turkey body.

2. Cut tail and wing feathers and a head and neck from poster board.

3. *Ask an adult to help you* make small slits at the front, back, and sides of the potato with a table knife. Gently slide the head and neck into the front slit. Slide the tail and wing feathers into the back and side slits. Add glue.

4. Cut a 2-inch ring from a bathroom tissue tube, paint it, and let it dry. Place the potato turkey on top of the ring.

THANKFULNESS CARD
(poster board, fallen leaf, construction paper)

1. Fold a piece of poster board in half. On the front, trace around a fallen leaf. Tear scraps of construction paper into small pieces, and glue them to fill the leaf shape.

2. Inside the card, write a message such as "Thank you for being there when I need you."

PILGRIM PUPPET
(small brown paper bag, paper)

1. Flatten a small brown paper bag. With paper and glue, make the girl's head, starting from her top lip to her hat, on the bottom of the paper bag.

2. Lift up the bag bottom. Cut and glue features for the bottom half of her hat, her mouth, and the rest of her body.

3. Place your hand inside the bag, and curve your fingers over the fold to move the puppet's head.

PHOTO MOUSE
(paper, photograph)

1. Cut out a 4-by-5-inch piece of paper. Cut the paper into three equal sections, as shown.

2. Fold the top section forward. Cut in 1/2 inch on the fold from each side (between the top and middle sections). With the top still folded forward, fold the curved ends up to meet in the center to form the head. Add eyes and a nose with a marker.

3. Cut paper whiskers, half-circles for inside the ears, and a strip for the tail. Glue them in place. Roll the end of the tail around a pencil to curve it.

4. Cut a paper circle for the mouse's belly. Glue it in place. Glue a photo to the center of it.

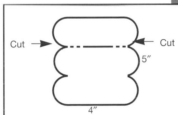

POPCORN HOLDER
(felt, round cardboard container with lid, rickrack)

1. Cut yellow felt and glue onto a round cardboard container. Cut out and glue other pieces of felt to create an ear of corn for a decoration.

2. Add rickrack around the top and bottom of the container.

3. Store kernels of popcorn in the container.

TALL TURKEY
(toothpaste box, brown wrapping paper, construction paper)

1. Cover a long toothpaste box with brown wrapping paper.

2. Cut eyes, a beak, a hat, and feet from construction paper. Attach them with glue.

3. Cut tail feathers from construction paper and glue to the back of the box.

HARVEST GARLAND
(paper, felt, straight pins, fabric glue, cotton balls, twine)

1. Draw vegetable and fruit shapes on paper and cut them out. Pin the shapes on pieces of felt with straight pins, and cut around them. Cut two pieces of felt for each fruit or vegetable shape.

2. Spread glue on the edges of one felt shape, and place a few cotton balls in the center. Place the second piece of felt on top of the first, pressing the pieces together at the edges. Add green felt pieces for leaves.

3. Glue or staple the decorations to a long piece of twine. Hang the garland over a door or window.

ICE-CREAM-STICK PUZZLE
(ice-cream sticks, masking tape, markers or crayons)

1. Place several ice-cream sticks together on your work surface. Place a strip of masking tape across all the sticks. Number the sticks in order, left to right.

2. Turn the sticks over. Draw a picture on them with markers or crayons. Remove the tape.

3. Mix up the sticks, and try to put the picture back together without looking at the numbers on the back.

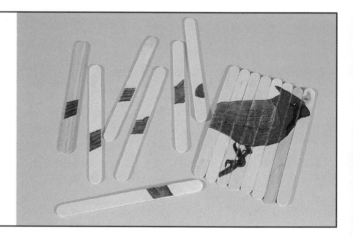

THANKSGIVING FAVOR
(paper towel tube, treats, brown wrapping paper, ribbon, cotton ball, construction paper)

1. For each favor, cut a 5-inch section from a paper towel tube. Place treats inside the tube.

2. Cut a piece of brown wrapping paper about 8 by 10 inches. Wrap the paper around the tube. Gather the ends and tie with a ribbon. Cut slits in the ends, making fringe. Glue a cotton ball for a head. Add features from construction paper.

3. For the tail, cut different-sized circles of yellow, black, and red construction paper, as shown. Fringe the edges of the circles and glue the circles on top of each other. Cut about 1/4 inch off the bottom so the tail is even. Glue the tail to the tube.

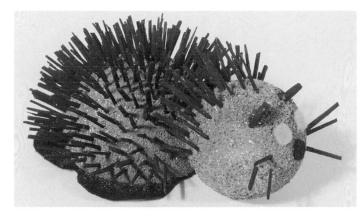

PORCUPINE
(3-inch plastic-foam ball, table knife, ice-cream stick,
2-inch plastic-foam ball, poster paint, sponge, felt, toothpicks)

1. To make the body, cut a 3-inch plastic-foam ball in half with a table knife. Place one of the halves in your supply box to use another time.

2. To make the head and neck, break an ice-cream stick in half. Put glue on one end of the stick, and push it into a 2-inch plastic-foam ball. Put glue on the other end of the stick and push it into the body.

3. Cover the body with poster paint, using a small piece of sponge. When dry, place the body on a piece of felt, and trace around it. Add four feet and a tail. Cut out the felt shape, and glue it to the body.

4. Break off the ends of one ice-cream stick. Paint them black. When dry, add glue and insert them in the head for ears. Cut out felt eyes and a nose, and glue to the head. Draw a mouth with a marker.

5. Paint some toothpicks black and let dry. Break them in half and insert them in the body. Add toothpick whiskers.

FESTIVE FRUIT CUP
(plastic cup, paper)

1. Create fruit designs, such as grapes, apples, and pears, on a plastic cup with cutout paper. Attach with glue.

2. Make a cup with different fruit on it for each dinner guest.

TONGUE DEPRESSOR PUPPET
(tempera paint, tongue depressor, permanent marker,
two moveable plastic eyes, construction paper, lightweight cardboard)

1. Paint a turkey body on a tongue depressor. Add a beak and feet with a permanent marker. Glue two moveable plastic eyes on the turkey.

2. Cut tail feathers from construction paper, and glue them to the back of the tongue depressor.

3. Glue a lightweight piece of cardboard in the shape of a ring to the back of the tongue depressor. When dry, place the puppet on your finger.

CHRYSANTHEMUM SCULPTURE
(poster paint, bathroom tissue tubes, yarn, paper)

1. Paint two bathroom tissue tubes and let dry.

2. For each tube, begin by cutting 1/2 inch from the end of the tube. Continue to cut around in a coil shape toward the other end of the tube. Bend the two ends of the coil together, and tie with a piece of yarn to form one flower.

3. Glue the flowers to a piece of paper. Add painted stems and leaves.

EGG-CARTON TURKEY
(cardboard egg carton, poster paint, lightweight cardboard, construction paper)

1. To make the body, cut two cups from a cardboard egg carton and glue them together. Paint when the glue is dry.

2. To make the tail feathers, cut another cup from the egg carton. Carefully cut a zigzag edge around the rim. Paint tail feathers. When dry, glue it to the body.

3. Cut out the neck and head from lightweight cardboard. Add details with paint. Cut a small slit in the body and glue the shape in place.

4. Add construction paper wings and feet.

SALT-AND-PEPPER PILGRIMS
(cardboard salt-and-pepper shakers, paper)

1. Decorate the sides of cardboard salt-and-pepper shakers with cut pieces of paper to make features and clothing for a Pilgrim boy and a Pilgrim girl.

2. Use markers to add eyes, noses, and mouths.

MARBLE BEETLE BUG
(heavyweight paper, small marble)

1. Draw a 4-inch-long shape, as shown, on heavyweight paper. Fold up the sides on the dotted lines. Overlap and tape the tabs together.

2. Roll each end of the center strip around a pencil to curve it. Wrap one end of the strip around the overlapped tabs. Tape in place.

3. Place a small marble inside. Wrap the other end of the center strip around the shape and tape in place. Decorate with markers. Give the bug a little push, and it will wobble back and forth.

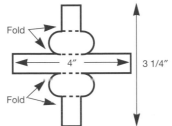

Fold
Fold
4″
3 1/4″

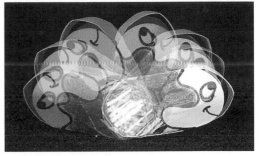

HOLIDAY GROCERY ENVELOPE
(envelope)

1. On the front of an envelope, draw a holiday design and straight black lines in the center, as shown.

2. List your holiday groceries on the lines. Place coupons inside the envelope.

SCARECROW WREATH
(fallen leaves, magazine, paper plate, ice-cream sticks, brown paper bag, yarn, fabric)

1. Place fallen leaves between magazine pages to press and dry for a few days. Cut the center from a paper plate, leaving a ring. Glue the dried leaves around the ring.

2. To make the scarecrow's body, glue two ice-cream sticks in an X shape. Glue another stick across the front of the X for arms. For the face, cut a circle from a brown paper bag. Glue yarn pieces to the ends of the arms and legs and to the head.

3. To make clothes, glue fabric around the legs for pants. Cut out a shirt. Glue it to the body.

4. To make a hat, cut a circle and a strip from the paper bag. Roll the strip and glue it to the center of the circle.

5. Glue the scarecrow to the wreath. Add a yarn hanger to the back.

WOODEN-SPOON PILGRIM
(paper, wooden spoon, fabric, yarn)

1. To make the head, cut eyes, a mouth, and hair from paper. Glue them to the inside of a wooden spoon. Cut a bonnet from paper and glue it to the outside of the wooden spoon.

2. To make the dress, cut an A-shaped piece of fabric and glue it around the spoon handle. Cut fabric arms and glue them to the back.

3. Add a collar, cuffs, hands, and apron from paper. Cut a small piece of yarn and make a bow. Glue it to the collar.

4. Attach a small piece of yarn to the back of the bonnet for a hanger.

TURKEY FOOD CLIP
(spring-type clothespin, paper)

1. For the head, cut a small circle from paper. Add paper eyes, a beak, and a wattle. Glue the head to one side of a spring-type clothespin.

2. Cut another small circle from paper. Add paper tail feathers around the edge. Glue the tail to the other side of the clothespin.

3. Cut a body from paper and glue it under the head. Draw legs and feet with a marker.

HOLIDAY POSTCARD
(paper, poster board)

1. Draw a fireplace scene similar to the way the Pilgrim home may have looked. Write a message such as "Good Wishes for Thanksgiving Day" in the lower corner.

2. Glue the picture on a piece of poster board that is slightly larger than the drawing to form a border. (The postal minimum size is 3 1/2 by 5 inches, the maximum size is 4 1/4 by 6 inches.)

3. On the back of the picture, draw a line to create a message area and address section. Add a stamp in the upper right-hand corner of the postcard.

Good Wishes for Thanksgiving Day

STUFFED TURKEY
(brown paper bag, construction paper, yarn, cotton balls, chenille stick)

1. Cut two 8-inch circles from a brown paper bag. Cut a slit in the middle of one circle. Insert a turkey's head made of construction paper. Tape in place.

2. Place the second circle behind the first circle. Punch holes around the edge of the circles, about 1 inch apart. Lace the circles together with a piece of yarn, leaving an opening. Stuff the turkey with cotton balls. Finish lacing, and tie the ends of the yarn together.

3. Cut tail feathers from construction paper, and glue them between the circles. Staple pieces of a chenille stick for feet.

PLASTIC-BOTTLE VASE
(plastic bottle, fabric)

1. Cut the top from a plastic bottle. Discard the top. Cut a curved edge on the bottom section.

2. Cover the outside of the bottle with scraps of fabric attached with glue.

FABRIC CAT
(paper, straight pins, fabric,
needle and thread, cotton balls, permanent markers)

1. Draw a simple cat design on paper. Cut it out. Use straight pins and pin the paper pattern on a folded piece of light-colored fabric. Cut around the pattern.

2. With the right sides of the fabric facing each other, sew around the edges, using a straight stitch. Leave the bottom open. Turn the fabric cat right-side out. Stuff the cat shape with cotton balls. Sew the bottom closed.

3. Using permanent markers, lightly draw details on the fabric.

Straight stitch

DRUMSTICK BOOKMARK
(paper)

1. Draw and cut out a turkey-drumstick shape. Color it with markers to create a "roasted" look.

2. Use the drumstick to keep your place in a recipe book.

THANKSGIVING BASKET
(brown paper bag, paper)

1. Place a folded brown paper bag flat on the table with the folded bottom of the bag facing up. Place your hand flat against the bag, with your wrist at the upper edge of the bag bottom. Trace around your hand onto the bag.

2. Without cutting the bottom of the bag, cut in from the sides of the bag to meet the wrist. Then cut around the traced hand (through both thicknesses of the bag).

3. Decorate the bag with markers.

4. Open the bag. To form handles, glue together the fingertips to make praying hands. Fill the bag with slips of paper listing things for which you are grateful.

ICE-CREAM-STICK TURKEY
(2-inch plastic-foam ball, tempera paint, 3-inch plastic-foam ball, ice-cream sticks, yarn, chenille stick, felt)

1. To make the head, cover a 2-inch plastic-foam ball with brown tempera paint. To make the body, cut a 3-inch plastic-foam ball in half and cover one half with brown paint. Save the other half for another project.

2. Insert 1 inch of an ice-cream stick into the center of the head. Poke 1 inch of the other end into the curved side of the body. Glue yarn around the stick.

3. Cut a 3-inch piece of chenille stick. Fold it in half and push the folded end into the face for a beak. Add felt eyes and a wattle.

4. Paint ice-cream sticks in different colors and let dry. Put glue on one stick end and insert them in the body for the tail feathers.

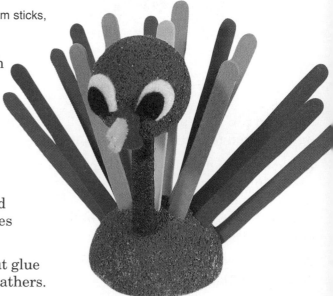

BLACK-BEAR SOCK TOY
(black sock, cotton balls, needle and thread, felt, buttons)

1. Cut off the leg of a black sock at the heel and discard. Stuff the foot portion with cotton balls and sew the bottom closed.

2. Shape the toe of the sock into a small ball. Tie a piece of thread at the bottom of the ball, forming the head and neck of a bear. With a needle and thread, stitch some of the head area together to form a snout. Glue a small piece of felt onto the end of the snout.

3. Sew two buttons to the head for eyes. Cut and sew two small felt ears. Cut out felt legs. Glue them to the bear.

PEAR-SHAPE TWIG WREATH
(twigs, rubber band, ribbon)

1. Take one long twig and bend it around in a pear shape. Hold it together with a small rubber band. Wrap other twigs around the pear frame, building up the wreath.

2. Wrap a long piece of ribbon around the wreath. Add a bow at the top. Attach a loop of ribbon for a hanger.

PLACE CARD
(cardboard egg carton, lightweight cardboard, tempera paint, chenille stick)

1. Cut a cup from a cardboard egg carton. Make the cut edges even.

2. Cut a head and tail shape from lightweight cardboard. Cut a slit in the bottom of the cup and insert the head in the slit.

3. Bend one chenille stick into a U shape. Glue the chenille stick to the bottom edge of the tail with the legs extending below. Then glue the cup to the tail, over the chenille-stick legs. Paint the turkey with tempera paint.

4. For the card, cut a rectangle from lightweight cardboard and paint it. Shape part of the chenille stick into feet. Glue the feet on top of the card.

5. Write a guest's name on the card.

SCRIBBLE TURKEY
(paper, cardboard egg carton, two beans)

1. On a sheet of paper, scribble circles with crayons of different colors to make one big semicircle. Leave room at the bottom of the paper.

2. Cut one cup from a cardboard egg carton. Glue the cup in the center of the bottom of the semicircle, as shown.

3. Cut a circle from paper and glue it onto the cup. Glue two beans for eyes. Add details with a marker. Cut a paper beak and wattle and glue in place. Draw legs and feet with a marker.

SQUIRREL NUT HOLDER
(half-gallon milk carton, paper)

1. Measure 2 inches from the bottom of a half-gallon milk carton, and draw a line around the outside of the carton. Cut along the line to make a small square box.

2. Glue paper to the outside of the box and about 1 inch inside the box. Draw and cut out a squirrel and glue it to the outside of the box. Fill with peanuts.

TURKEY GOBBLER
(paper towel tube, two paper plates, paper)

1. Hold one end of a paper towel tube against a paper plate, and trace around it. Cut out the circle on the plate. Lay the plate on top of another plate, trace around the hole, and cut out the circle on the second plate.

2. Cut five slits in the end of the paper towel tube, and bend the pieces flat. Slip the tube through the hole in one paper plate, and tape the bent pieces tightly to the plate, as shown in the diagram.

3. Using the hole as the turkey's mouth, add cut-paper eyes, a beak, and a wattle to the back of the second paper plate. Cut and glue tail feathers around the rim of the plate. Add legs and feet.

4. Place the second paper plate over the first one, with the holes lining up. Staple the rims together.

5. Put the paper towel tube to your mouth, and gobble like a turkey.

HORN OF PLENTY
(small brown paper bag, modeling clay, paper)

1. Roll down the top few inches of a small brown paper bag. Twist the paper bag tightly from bottom to top. At the top, gently open the bag to form a cone shape.

2. Use modeling clay to mold various fruits and vegetables. Cut different-colored fall leaves from paper.

3. Lay the bag on its side in the middle of a table. Place the fruits and leaves in the opening of the bag.

BRAIDED COASTER
(yarn, thread, straight pins)

1. Cut nine lengths of yarn, three each of three different colors, about a yard long. Group the same colors together. Lining them up lengthwise, tie the groups together with thread at one end, as shown.

2. Braid by folding Group 1 over Group 2, and then Group 3 over Group 1, as shown. Continue until the whole length is braided. Glue the ends together.

3. Starting at one end, curl the braid into a flat coil. As the coil is being formed, add small amounts of glue to the edges of the braid to hold it. Use straight pins to help keep the coil together until it is dry.

PINE SACHET
(fresh pine, fabric, pinking shears, rickrack)

1. *Ask an adult to help you* pick some small sprigs or needles of fresh pine.

2. Cut two 5-inch-square pieces of fabric with pinking shears to get a saw-toothed effect.

3. Place the pine in the center of one square. Squeeze glue around the edges of the fabric. Place the second piece of fabric on top and press the fabric into the glue.

4. Cut pieces of rickrack and glue to one side of the sachet for decoration.

HARVEST BREADBOARD
(corrugated cardboard, tempera paint)

1. Cut a breadboard shape from heavy corrugated cardboard, as shown. Cover it with brown tempera paint.

2. Paint the word "Harvest" on the bottom of the board. Add harvest decorations such as wheat, a pumpkin, and apples.

3. Punch a hole at the top of the board to hang.

FALL-TREE CARD
(paper, old newspaper, sponge, tempera paint)

1. Fold a piece of paper in half to make a card. Spread old newspaper on your work surface. Open the card.

2. Cut a soft sponge into small pieces. Dip pieces of the sponge in various colors of tempera paint. Lightly touch the paper with the sponges to create a fall tree on the front of the card.

CLAY-POT PLANTER
(clay flower pot and base, acrylic paint;
high-gloss, waterbased crystal-clear glaze)

1. Cover a clay flower pot and base with a white acrylic paint. Let dry overnight.

2. Lightly sketch wheat around the flower pot. With a brush, paint the wheat a golden color. Paint a ring around the base. Let dry.

3. To protect the flower pot, *ask an adult to help you* cover it with a clear glaze, following the package directions.

PERKY TURKEY
(bathroom tissue tube, tempera paint)

1. Cut 2 1/2-inch-deep slits, spaced about 1/4 inch apart, around a bathroom tissue tube. Leave the last two spaces wider with 3-inch-deep slits for the legs.

2. Cut 1 inch from each leg, then cut talon shapes on the ends. Bend the talons at right angles, then bend the feet as shown, 1/2 inch from the end. Spread out the slit sections to form tail feathers.

3. Cut 3/4-inch slits on the front of the tube at the center top and bottom. Draw and cut out a cardboard head. Insert it into the slits.

4. Cover the turkey with tempera paints.

HOLIDAY HAND TOWEL
(terry-cloth hand towel, rickrack, fabric glue, felt, needle, embroidery floss)

1. Decorate a terry-cloth hand towel by attaching rickrack with fabric glue along the flat woven band on the towel. Let dry.

2. Cut a felt apple, leaf, and pear. Attach the felt pieces to the towel with fabric glue. Let dry.

3. With a needle and embroidery floss, sew a single featherstitch design, as shown, around the outside of the felt pieces.

Single featherstitch

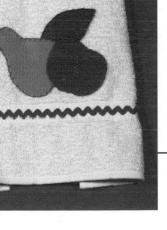

CLOTHESPIN PILGRIMS
(paint, clothespins, paper)

1. Paint the very top of two clothespins with facial features of a Pilgrim man and Pilgrim woman.

2. Paint arms and clothing details on the rest of the clothespins. Paint the tips of the clothespins to make shoes.

3. To make the man's hat, cut a small black-paper circle. Cut a small strip of paper and glue the ends together to form a ring. Glue the ring on its edge to the circle.

4. To make the woman's bonnet, cut a small white rectangle and glue it to her head.

PILGRIM HARVEST CENTERPIECE
(cookie sheet, construction paper, nuts, vegetables, fruits, berries, twigs, walnuts, yarn)

1. Line the bottom of a cookie sheet with green construction paper. Arrange nuts, vegetables, fruits, and berries along the edges of the sheet. Place leaves cut from construction paper on the sheet.

2. Break twigs into small pieces. Glue them together for a "cookfire" in the center of the sheet. Cut and glue red and orange flames to the twigs.

3. To make the Pilgrim bodies, cut a paper circle. Make a slit to the center of the circle and pull the ends together to form a cone.

4. To make the heads, decorate walnuts with markers, yarn, and paper. Let the ridge dividing the halves be the nose. Glue the heads to the top of the cones. Place the Pilgrims around the fire.

SOAP TURKEY
(bar of soap, table knife, construction paper, toothpicks)

1. For the body of the turkey, *ask an adult to help you* round off each corner of a bar of soap with a table knife. The bottom should be flat.

2. Cut wing and tail feathers from construction paper and glue each feather to a toothpick. When dry, stick the toothpick feathers in place on the turkey body.

3. To make the head, cut two turkey shapes from construction paper. Glue them together with a toothpick neck between the two shapes. Stick the head and neck on the body.

THANKSGIVING PLACE CARD
(small paper cup, tempera paint, construction paper, index card)

1. Cover a small paper cup with brown tempera paint. Cut two side-by-side slits, 1/2 inch apart, in the bottom of the cup.

2. Cut rows of connected feathers from red, orange, and yellow construction paper, making each row a different size. Glue the largest feathers to the back of the cup. Glue the base of the medium-sized feathers in the slit nearest the back. Glue the base of the smallest feathers in the other slit.

3. Draw and cut out a paper turkey's head. Add eyes and a beak with a marker. Glue the head to the front of the cup.

4. Glue the turkey to an index card on which you've written the name of the person the turkey is for. Add something about that person for which you're thankful.

DAD
Thanks for coaching me! xoxo

POTATO BAG

(fabric, needle and thread, felt, string, safety pin)

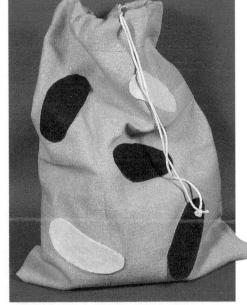

1. Cut a piece of fabric. (See Diagram 1.)

2. Open the fabric and fold over a hem of 2 inches. With a needle and thread sew a running stitch along the hem. (See Diagram 2.)

3. Fold the fabric wrong-side out with the edges touching and the hem at the top. Then sew along the bottom and up the side just to the hem. (See Diagram 3.)

4. Turn the bag right-side out. Cut a piece of string three times the width of the bag. Attach a large safety pin to one end of the string. Thread it through one opened end of the hem and come out the other end. Remove the safety pin and tie the ends of the string together. (See Diagram 4.)

5. Cut and glue felt potatoes on the bag. To close the bag, pull the string toward you and push the fabric away from you.

 Running stitch

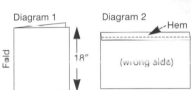

Diagram 1 Diagram 2 ←Hem Diagram 3 Diagram 4

Fold 18″ (wrong side) (wrong side) (right side)

← 14″ →

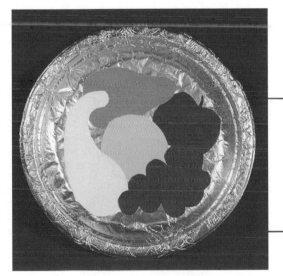

HOLIDAY SERVING PLATE

(heavy paper plate, aluminum foil, paper)

1. Cover a heavy paper plate with aluminum foil. Cut fruit and vegetable shapes from paper. Glue the shapes onto the center of the plate.

SUNFLOWER SPINNER

(poster board, paper plate, sunflower seeds, yarn)

1. Draw and cut a flower from yellow poster board. Cut two circles from the poster board and glue them to the center on each side of the flower.

2. Squeeze a little glue on a paper plate. Holding the pointed end of a sunflower seed, dip the flat end in the glue. Place the seed upright on the circle. Fill the circle with seeds, let dry, then fill the circle on the other side with seeds.

3. Punch a hole in one petal of the flower. Tie a piece of yarn for a hanger. Hang the flower where it can spin around.

HARVEST BRACELET
(plastic ribbon ring, fabric ribbon, poster board)

1. For the bracelet, use a plastic ring that holds ribbon. Cover the outside of the ring with glue and fabric ribbon for the base. Cover this with another color of fabric ribbon.

2. Cut various fruits from poster board and glue on top of the ribbon.

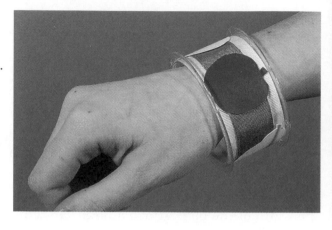

GOURD PILGRIM
(ornamental gourd, paper)

1. Look for an ornamental gourd that could be made into a head of a Pilgrim.

2. Cut a hat, as shown, and glue in place. Cut paper eyes and a mouth. Glue to the gourd. One of the bumps on the gourd could be the nose.

RING THE GOOSE
(corrugated cardboard, fuzzy white fabric, moveable plastic eyes, string, plastic lid)

1. Draw and cut a goose shape from a piece of corrugated cardboard. Place the goose on a fuzzy white fabric and trace around it twice. Cut out the two geese. Glue one to each side of the cardboard goose. Attach a moveable plastic eye to each side of the goose's head with glue.

2. Punch a hole in the breast of the goose. Tie a long string to the hole.

3. Cut the center from a plastic lid, leaving a ring. Attach the other end of the string to the ring.

4. Hold the tail of the goose and try to swing the ring up and around the goose's neck.

TURKEY CENTERPIECE
(two paper plates, construction paper)

1. Fold a paper plate in half. Color it with markers or crayons to look like a turkey's body. Draw and color wings.

2. Using another paper plate, cut as shown, creating a tail-feather section. Color feathers on both sides of the plate. Make the center section of the plate brown.

3. Cut two heads from construction paper. Glue them together and add eyes, a beak, and a wattle. Slide the head into a 1-inch slit along the fold line of the body and add glue.

4. Two inches from the back of the body, cut a slit, slanting it toward the front. Insert the tail in the slit.

JACK FROST
(fallen leaf, paper plate, yarn)

1. To make the body, glue an autumn leaf to the center of a paper plate. Add arms, legs, and a face with markers.

2. Glue the tip of a second autumn leaf to the top of the head for a cap.

3. Add a yarn bow tie and a loop of yarn glued to the back of the paper plate for a hanger.

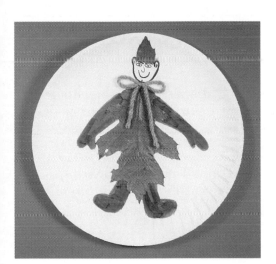

LEAF SWEAT SHIRT
(cardboard, white sweat shirt, fabric paint)

1. Draw and cut out a leaf shape from the center of a piece of cardboard, making a stencil. Create several different leaf stencils.

2. Lay a washed sweat shirt flat on your work surface. Put a large piece of cardboard inside the sweat shirt.

3. Think of a design you want, and tape a stencil on one section of the sweat shirt. Paint the inside of the stencil with fabric paint. Gently lift the stencil from the fabric. Select another stencil and another color of paint and repeat. Continue until the sweat shirt is covered with leaves.

4. Follow the directions on the paint bottle for drying time.

Corn Creations

Corn was a staple of the Pilgrims' diet and was served during their first Thanksgiving. Here are holiday decorations you can create with it.

DOOR DECORATION
(ornamental corn, string, ribbon, poster board)

1. Gather small ears of corn with their husks still attached, and tie them into bunches with string. Leave a loop of string in the back.

2. Tie a large ribbon over the string.

3. Cut various colored leaves from poster board. Glue them within the ribbon folds. Attach the corn to a door with the string loop.

KERNEL SIGN
(poster board, corn kernels, yarn)

1. Cut a piece of poster board and scallop the edges. Cut another piece of poster board of a different color and glue onto the first. Glue a small leaf cut from poster board in the center.

2. Lightly sketch the letters on the poster board to spell "Happy Autumn." Glue corn kernels on top of the letters. Let dry.

3. Tape a piece of yarn to the back and hang the sign.

DRIED-HUSK FLOWER
(dried cornhusk, green poster board, dried corn silk, dried corn kernels)

1. Glue dried pieces of cornhusk on a piece of green poster board in a flower design.

2. In the center of the flower, glue dried corn silk. Using dried corn kernels, glue them in the center of the corn silk, making a design. Let dry overnight.

3. Trim around the flower with scissors, cutting a flower design in the poster board. Place the flower in the center of a table.

WOVEN MAT
(dried cornhusks, warm water, paper towels, poster board)

1. To make dried cornhusks easy to handle, soak them in warm water for about five minutes. Remove and drain. Place them on paper towels to dry slightly.

2. Cut a piece of poster board about 8 1/2 by 11 inches. Cut and glue sections of cornhusk together, making long strips, as shown.

3. Glue one cornhusk strip vertically and one horizontally in the corner of the poster board. Add more strips, weaving them over and under each other. Cut and glue down the ends of the strips.

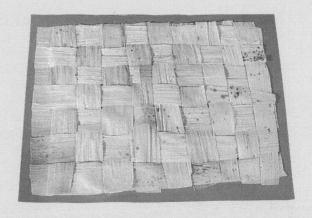

Strips

CORNHUSK BRACELET
(dried cornhusks, warm water, paper towels, leather shoelace)

1. To make dried cornhusks easy to handle, soak them in warm water for about five minutes. Remove and drain. Place them on paper towels to dry slightly.

2. Cut and glue sections of cornhusks together, making long strips. Let dry.

3. Tie the ends of three strips together with a small piece of leather shoelace. Braid the cornhusk strips by folding 1 over 2, and then 3 over 1, as shown. Continue until the whole length is braided. Tie the other end together with another small piece of leather shoelace.

4. To wear the bracelet, tie the laces together.

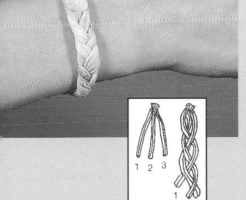

CORNHUSK PILGRIM
(dried cornhusks, yarn, dried corn silk, paper, felt)

1. To make the body, gather dried cornhusks together. Tie a piece of yarn around them about 2 1/4 inches down from one end.

2. Glue dried corn silk to the top for hair.

3. Cut a piece of felt and glue it around the cornhusks to form a dress. Add a paper collar, apron, and hat. Cut two felt arms. Add paper cuffs. Cut hand shapes from cornhusks and glue in place.

4. Add cut-paper features to the face.

MATERIAL INDEX